the vicious kind

Krysta Fitzpatrick

Published in Canada by Engen Books, Chapel Arm, NL.

Library and Archives Canada Cataloguing in Publication information is available on the publisher's website.

ISBN-13: 978-1-77478-166-1

Copyright © 2024 Krysta Fitzpatrick

NO PART OF THIS BOOK MAY BE REPRODUCED OR TRANSMITTED IN ANY FORM OR BY ANY MEANS, ELECTRONIC OR MECHANICAL, INCLUDING PHOTOCOPYING AND RECORDING, OR BY ANY INFORMATION STORAGE OR RETRIEVAL SYSTEM WITHOUT WRITTEN PERMISSION FROM THE AUTHOR, EXCEPT FOR BRIEF PASSAGES QUOTED IN A REVIEW.

Distributed by:
Engen Books
www.engenbooks.com
submissions@engenbooks.com

First mass market paperback printing: November 2024

Cover Images: Shan Leigh Pomeroy

the vicious kind

Krysta Fitzpatrick

"They say a woman's first blood doesn't come from between her legs
but from biting her tongue."
- Meggie Royer

This book is a work of fiction.
Each piece is its own,
with no consistent narrator.
None of the following is true,
except the parts that actually happened.

Hunger: An Inventory of Girlhood and Abjection

Nails.
When I was in the 6th grade,
my friends Danielle, Maria, and I would grow our nails out,
paint them wild colours,
then pierce the tips.
We would buy cheap packs of studded earrings at the dollar store,
then go out in Maria's backyard after school and force the earrings
through the tips of our fingernails.
I very specifically liked to wear little fake silver crosses.
Danielle always wore hearts on her thumbs,
and,
for the life of me,
I can't remember what Maria preferred.
But we did this every couple of weeks.
Eventually our nails would get too long, and we'd have to trim them.
Then we'd have to paint and pierce all over again.
 I would do mine in black and draw little designs with a silver Sharpie.
Then I'd put in the silver crosses.
Keep in mind this was 1997 and the movie The Craft was very significant to me.
Also keep in mind this was St. John's, Newfoundland,
not New York or London,
or somewhere else maybe a girl could express herself through fashion.
Aside from the nails, I also regularly wore black lipstick.
I felt very strongly about my aesthetic,
and every day before school I would look in the mirror and like what stared back at me.
One day, I was sitting in math class when the boy who sat in front of me turned around and stared at me for what felt like a very long time.
His name was Craig.

"What?" I asked.
"Why do you do your nails like that?"
"Like what?"
"Like all black, and with earrings through them. It's weird."
"No, it isn't," I said, though,
surprisingly, I didn't feel so sure.
"Yeah, it is. And so is black lipstick. You shouldn't wear that stuff. It doesn't look good."
Then he turned around.
That was it.
After that I stopped piercing my nails and wearing black lipstick.

Voice.
Every year in school,
all students had to take part in public speaking during English class.
We all had to write our own speeches and present them.
Some people wrote about their dog who had passed away
or their favourite hockey players.
There were two speeches about the importance of Wayne Gretzky.
I had just seen the Demi Moore movie *G.I. Jane* and it inspired me to write a speech about feminism.
I was only 12,
but I went to the local library and did some research.
I read Simone de Beauvoir and Audre Lorde.
I read Betty Friedan and bell hooks.
I loved writing,
I loved speaking,
and I was passionate about the topic.
I gave an emotional speech about gender inequality, sexism, and oppression.
When I was done my female English teacher clapped enthusiastically.
Most of the class gave me some light golf claps.
Some of the boys did not clap at all.
They just looked at me.
They looked at me the same way they looked at Lauren Parsons when she got her first period in class and bled through her pants.

How dare she reveal herself like that in front of them.
After that I stopped talking about feminism and women's issues.

Body.
I wasn't a late bloomer.
I got my first period when I was 11,
and for the first hour of it I was thrilled.
You forget that as time passes,
but before you actually get it,
you are so excited about starting your period.
In the months leading up to getting mine,
I would carry panty liners with me everywhere and subtly show my girlfriends that I had them.
I was one of the first girls in my friend group to get their period,
and this made me feel very special for a whole hour.
Once the reality of what a period was set in,
the glamour faded.
I had expected breasts and other womanly things to follow once I started bleeding,
but nothing happened.
My anxiety increased and I began chewing down my nails.
My throat ached and my voice faltered.
I stayed a scrawny 60 pounds.
While the other girls started requiring real bras,
I barely needed the training bra I wore religiously.
At the pool that summer,
I wore a pink polka dot bikini that I had begged my mother to buy me.
I got to the park early to get in line for the pool,
as it was always packed.
I brought my donut inner tube with me to float on because I wasn't a great swimmer.
It was unusually hot out that day and I couldn't wait to get in the water.
Finally, they let us all in.
Back then it was a buck twenty-five to swim at Bowring Park,
now it's free.
As I was getting my things set up on a pool chair, Dean Hobbs, a boy

from our school who was a year older than us, walked by and looked me up and down.
He snickered and told me to go "find a fridge."
My girlfriends laughed, too.
How could they not?
He was older and more popular than us.
After that,
I never wore a bikini in public again.

Skin.
Time passed and I forgot about all the things I used to do.
I forgot about my writing and my feminism and my black nail polish.
I barely left the house, aside from school.
My skin got paler,
and my lips and nails turned an odd hue of blue.
I bought Cover Girl foundation in a shade darker than my natural skin.
I purchased a nude pink lipstick, and started painting my nails a cherry red.
When my face began to look gaunt and hollow,
I bought a pretty peach blush to apply to the little bit of fat that sat on the apples of my cheeks.
This, mixed with the too dark foundation, always made me look just a little bit sun-kissed.
I applied thick layers of mascara.
I always looked drowsy because my eyelashes were so heavy.
I thought I looked like Marilyn Monroe.
I had stayed in track—it was the one thing I enjoyed that didn't seem to bother anyone,
but after a while I had no choice but to quit.
I just couldn't move that fast anymore.
I couldn't focus.
I could hear the teaching speaking and read the numbers on the chalkboard, but they stopped making sense to me.
I started getting simple equations wrong.
My stomach would moan,
and I could smell the sweat of the boy sitting in front of me.
I could smell copper.

I could smell his thoughts.
But I couldn't do fractions anymore.
I'd stare off into space and when I'd snap out of it, class would be over.
I wasn't connected with my body anymore,
and I'd watch as other people moved and breathed and existed,
and I couldn't help but wonder: am I still doing that?
Flies begin to pick at my scalp.
Not everywhere,
just on the spots where hair had begun to fall out.
No one noticed,
not even my parents.
I'd come home after school and examine the new empty,
fleshy spots on my head.
I'd pick at the fly bites with my cherry nails until they began to ooze.
I saved up my allowance and went to the beauty shop downtown.
I bought hideous clip in extensions and extra strength hairspray.
Every morning, I'd get up at 5am and clip in my hair and spray over the fly infested bald spots.
Then I'd put on my fake eyelashes, so no one would notice my real ones had fallen out.

Completion.
Everyone thinks I'm really pretty now,
and no one ever brings up that stupid speech I wrote or how I used to pierce my fingernails.
I guess I used to enjoy public speaking,
but I can't really speak anymore.
I can't wear fun nail polish either since my nails are gone.
I just put cherry coloured nail polish on the fleshy bits where they used to be,
like blood-tipped knubs.
No one seems to notice.
Popular boys talk to me all the time now and tell me all about themselves.
I sit there and listen and smile as much as I can.
They like me because I'm pretty and I never talk about myself.
I just sit there quietly and stare at them.

They think I'm such a good listener,
but really,
I can't stop thinking about how good their flesh might taste.

Lies My Mother Told Me

I think I always knew it would end like this.
Surrounded, yet alone.
It's how I've spent my whole life, really.
They say that no man is an island,
and perhaps they mean that.
But I assure you, no one has ever said that about a woman.
Women are islands off the coast of Man.
We can still be seen from the shore.
We are often still
considered a part of the mainland,
but we aren't really a part of it, are we?
We stand alone,
seen from a distance,
but barely heard,
left out on world maps.
Tiny islands claimed by bigger lands,
left to stand alone.
My mother always said you couldn't believe a word I said.
Not that I was a liar,
more so that I was intensely hyperbolic.
An unreliable narrator, of sorts.
Then again,
as I would often say to my mother,
we are all unreliable narrators in the grand scheme of reality.
And it is because of this reasoning that I don't consider my mother a
liar, either.
Maybe it's why I don't consider anyone a liar,
in some sense.
Years ago, I read somewhere that if a crime occurred and there were 50
eyewitnesses, the eyewitnesses alone would be insufficient evidence to

prosecute someone.
No one remembers things the same.
That doesn't make anyone's recollection wrong,
but it also makes everyone's recollection wrong.

So, I've forgiven my mother
for only telling me what she thought was the truth,
even if it wasn't.
Growing up,
I was always a bit uncomfortable with myself.
I'm not sure why.
I guess I just always thought I was weird,
and that I should probably just hide myself away.
Bury all the darkness deep down.
When I was a bit older,
I explained to someone that I tended to hide myself away from others,
and I think that they told me:
"It gets awfully lonely keeping yourself to yourself."
Or maybe no one told me that.
Maybe I just made it up myself.
Unreliable narration,
like I said.

It wasn't until I had children that I began to
consider all the lies we tell ourselves
and each other.
My mother lied to me a lot,
and I will never know whether that was intentional.
When I was young,
she would lie about our family and heritage.
I really knew nothing about us,
other than that we were all mentally ill alcoholics.
Kind of like the Hemingways
only poor.
My mother lied the most about her own mother.
My grandmother had an unremarkable nose.

Whenever I read descriptions about older women in books,
they go to painstaking length to describe the nose,
as if it's the most important part of the face simply because it is at the center.
Her nose was not beak-like and strong,
or round like a button.
It did not turn up at the end like a Disney princess,
nor was it flat and broad.
It was a nose and it existed above her thin lips,
and below her hooded eyes.
She had no eyelashes.
I never thought to ask why.
My grandmother's name was either Jeanette or Jane.
She was either born in 1922 or 1924.
She might have been born in rural Quebec,
she might have been born in Downtown St. John's.
I have been told varying accounts.
My mother lied to me about our socioeconomic status,
but I can understand that.
I didn't know we lived in a poor neighbourhood until I was much older,
and I suppose that's a good thing.
Perhaps the worst lie my mother ever told me was when I was pregnant with my first child.
She would put her hands on my large belly and tell me that there was no greater joy in the world than being a mother.
She told me that nothing would make me happier than my children,
nothing would feel so rewarding,
nothing would make me feel so connected to my womanhood.
It was her cruelest lie,
and I suppose I will never understand it,
or be able to forgive her.
After my first son was born,
I spent the first 6 months feeling too anxious to be alone with him.
On the days my husband worked I would go to my mother's house,
or my sister's apartment,
or even just walk around the mall for hours,

pushing him in his stroller,
just to avoid sitting home alone with him.
I slept at my mothers on nights my husband worked.
I'd put my baby in his playpen next to my childhood bed,
and my mother's new treadmill.
We would sleep in a room that looked like a home I remembered,
but felt overwhelmingly strange.
I didn't feel comfortable at home,
but I didn't feel comfortable anywhere else either.
I felt like I didn't belong anywhere.
Having a baby felt like I was trying to find space and place in a world that suddenly had no room.
Even when things are quiet and the sun is shining,
a part of me is still grieving.
I have measured my life in miserable summers.
The summers that hurt the most.
The summers that have burned in my veins and tore out my heart.
I mourned myself daily.
The woman I was,
the woman I thought I would be.
I mourned my personhood.
I mourned my identity,
my flat stomach,
my perky breasts.
I mourned my nights out dancing,
my spontaneous trips,
my combed hair.
I mourned silence and hot, slow cups of coffee.
I tried to put my feelings into words.
I needed someone to understand,
I began to tell anyone who would listen.
I began to scream the truth.
I don't want to be treated as a mother. I want to be treated as a woman!
I want to be good for my family, but still live my life recklessly!
I love my family, but I hate my life!
I am tired! I am angry! I am incapable of joy!

I have suffered,
but I was shamed in my suffering.
How dare you feel this pain?
They would say.
So many women would kill to be in your position. So many others have suffered so much more,
they would tell me,
as if pain were a competition.
I knew there were whispers.
I knew I had spoken the truth too loudly, and there would be repercussions.
There is no greater joy.
My mother's words echoed through my head on the day they came for me.
I should have known.
It all makes sense,
I thought,
as they dragged me to the town square.
They bound my arms behind me,
and the wood splintered into my skin.
The flames had not yet reached my toes,
but I could feel the rising heat.
I tried to spot my mother in the crowd,
but couldn't.

Collections

I started purchasing magnets when I was sixteen.
There was a little shop downtown called Posie Row, and they sold this and that.
Hand made earrings.
Postcards.
Teacups.
Candles.
Random things no one really needed but liked to have.
They had a big stand covered in magnets.
Some were clever, some were vulgar, some had old TV show pictures on them.
For some reason, I took to buying them.
I avoided buying vulgar ones because my deeply Catholic mother would not have approved me putting those on the fridge.
My absolute favourite magnets were the Anne Taintor ones.
The one I liked best had a woman in pink staring deadpan out at you that read "Maybe I want to look cheap." That one really got me.
I bought the magnet, a mug, a postcard, and a journal that I never used with that picture on it.
When I got married many years later, my mother bought me a little book of Anne Taintor art that I thought was very nice.
Especially since my mother didn't remember much about me.
I never lost my love of buying magnets.
When I moved out on my own, I started buying the vulgar magnets.
Real party conversation pieces.
I like to pick up magnets whenever I travel.
I purchased magnets in London, Paris, Venice, Amsterdam, Brazil, Georgia, Iceland, and, of course, Disney World.
They didn't have to be specific to the place I am, they mostly just have to amuse me.

They have to catch my eye.
I picked up a fun "Kate's Kitchen" magnet at a yard sale once even though I don't know anyone named Kate. I saw a magnet that was just a picture of Shirley Jackson when I was in this little bookstore in France and I knew I had to have it.
I didn't buy a Big Ben or Buckingham Palace magnet in London, but I did buy an oversized Star Trek one.
Anyone can pick up a souvenir that says where they've been.
Almost as important as the magnets themselves are the things that the magnets hold up on my fridge.
When I lived with my mother, I would stick up fun postcards I collected,
old family Polaroids,
positive funny messages for us to read.
When I moved out with my girlfriends, what the magnets held — much like the magnets themselves — got a bit more risqué.
There was a church flyer with a cartoon picture of Jesus nailed to the cross with a caption "Jesus Loves You So Much It Hurts."
It had been a gift from a boy I'd been sleeping with.
We had found an STD pamphlet from the 1980s and stuck it to our fridge.
We would put up the labels I carefully peeled off beer bottles to write lyrics on.
Which was painfully pretentious.
We'd put up Valentine's cards from our many lovers.
The entire fridge was a conversation piece; we would have parties and people would gather around and inquire into each piece of our unusual puzzle.
Eventually, I got older and married.
I had to share my fridge with a man for the first time, but that was ok.
My husband let me keep all my magnets up
though I had to get rid of the business cards and Valentines from other men.
And I was content.
Once we had children,
we decided it was best if I took my crass magnets down and put them

in a drawer in the kitchen.
I had a magnet with a grumpy looking frog on it that read "I'm so happy I could just shit."
It wasn't appropriate to have up once we had children.
After a while, the fridge was taken over by finger paintings,
school pictures,
and family Christmas cards from other friends who had married and fled to the safety of the suburbs.
After a while, we had so many kids that we had to move into a big house with too many bedrooms on a nice quiet street filled with doctors and lawyers and accountants.
The new house had a fridge so big it took up the space of two fridges.
I had been so impressed, and a little overwhelmed.
"Do we really need a fridge this big?"
The new fridge was ridiculously fancy.
It was some type of expensive stainless steel that was not magnetic.
I put my magnets in a shoe box.
I could not think of one single place I could possibly stick them.
I tucked them up on the top shelf of my closet,
thinking I would eventually find a place to put them again someday.
But I never did.

Where Strawberries Grow

Over the fence—
Strawberries— grow—
Over the fence—
I could climb—if I tried, I know—
Berries are nice!

But—if I stained my Apron—
God would certainly scold!
Oh, dear, — I guess if He were a Boy—
He'd—climb—if He could!
- Emily Dickinson

A gentle pain spreads through the right side of my abdomen. It nudges me until I am awake.
It moves and radiates, then goes away once I am up, out of bed, and moving.
This morning, my thighs feel stiff.
I wonder if these discomforts are connected.
Breakfast has been my sole responsibility since my twelfth birthday four months ago.
My father said I was the woman of the house now.
"If I'm the woman of the house now, does that mean I can go into town to do the shopping?"
He looked at my brothers and the three of them laughed.
The responsibilities of womanhood, but no added freedom.

I live in Newfoundland—or so I am told.
We have a nice, two-story white house, and a small farm with three sheep, a ram, a dairy cow, six chickens, three cats, an old hound dog, and a rooster.

We grow tomatoes, lettuce, red and green peppers, radishes, and carrots.
Five of the six acres belonging to my father are wooded, and the edge of the property is lined with a tall fence that I have never been beyond.
My brothers move freely amongst the trees, bushes, and hidden paths. They laugh and run into the woods, knowing I cannot follow.
I knew they had built a treehouse in there somewhere. They tease me about it when my father wasn't listening.
It was high off the ground and had chocolate bars they had bought in town.
They had put up pictures of naked girls from magazines they'd gotten from friends.
"I wouldn't want to go in your stinkin' club house anyway!" I shout, lying
Even if I had been allowed to go into the woods, the treehouse would still have been off limits for me. I am not allowed to climb trees.
The pain in my abdomen radiates, I must be dying.
Some nights in the summertime I would hear Matthew and Lucas sneak out after my father had gone to sleep.
I hated and envied my brothers.
I was not allowed out after dark.
I could sit on the porch with Bruce, our hound dog, but I could go no further.
I butter the toast.
My brothers have already milked Maggie, our cow, and collected eggs from the chickens that I never bothered to name.
I cook the eggs sunny side up and plate them alongside the thick slices of toast.
The kitchen smells of burnt coffee and cat urine.
Two similar scents.
I pour my father a cup, which he doesn't thank me for.
I have been taking a mental inventory of all the things no one thanks me for,
and I wonder if they would thank my mother if she were here.
Both of my brothers smoke cigarettes, which is fine at any age if you're a boy.
I know they drink some of my father's whiskey, too, but the appropriate age for that isn't quite so clear.

After breakfast is done and my brothers are gone, I clean up the dishes, feed the animals, and mop the main floor of the house.
On Wednesdays I dust, and on Sundays I clean the bathroom and do the laundry.
I asked my father once why we didn't grow fruit, and he just shrugged.
Sometimes my brothers bring home bags of apples from the grocery market.
I'm told tomato is a fruit, but I find them a stark contrast to apples.
The pain in my abdomen radiates, I'm sure I must be dying.
I wait for the pain to take over my entire body and carry my innocent soul off to my mother, but nothing happens.
I lay sprawled across my bed with my hand laid gently to my forehead, hoping that I will look very dramatic when my father finds my body.
But alas, I do not die.
My father is out past the barn digging a hole.
One of the cats died.
Cats are very disturbing creatures.
They viciously kill other animals — sometimes even beheading them — then bring it to the door and leave it, drenched in its own guts and blood, and mean it to be a gift.
It's midday.
The sun is shining, and the sky is clear.
The birds are singing.
My father is tending to the animals, and everything seems safe.
I begin to walk.
I take one step. Then another. And another.
I don't think I've ever been this far before.
I pause again and listen for the sounds of the farm.
I can still hear them, so I decide to go a bit further.
After a few minutes, the trees have eaten me up and I can no longer see my house.
I have never been this far, but I'm not scared.
The further I go, the darker it gets, as whisps of sunlight break through the sturdy branches of flush trees.
The sounds of the farm are behind me, now all I hear is the sound of my feet cracking over twigs and stomping over grass.

It is quiet, but satisfying.
I ponder it for a moment,
then feel certain that this is the only time in my entire life that I have felt truly alone.
I stand in the quiet of the trees and listen.
The only noise is the sound of wind lightly flickering through the trees.
Why would they deny me of this?
I feel betrayed, which is a sensation I have mostly only read about, but never experienced.
I sit with my feelings of treachery.
The pain in my abdomen radiates, I'm sure I must be dying.
I have always been told not to go into the woods because it wasn't safe.
Just like going to school wasn't safe.
Going into town wasn't safe.
Going out after dark wasn't safe.
It was safe for my brothers, but not for me.
"If I can't see you, I can't keep you safe."
The sun begins to set, and I lie in the grass tracing the dull pain in my abdomen.
I lie next to a bush covered in unusual red blobs.
I pluck one of the bloody lumps from the vine and sniff it.
It smells fresh, but also oddly caramel-like.
I squeeze the object gently.
It is juicy and sticky in my hand.
I hold it up close to my face and notice the little dots that cover it.
Though I am unsure of what it is, I am confident that it is edible.
I decide to try it.
I bite in, and it is firm and moist.
Sweet, but also bitter.
An abrasive yet pleasant taste.
I eat it up until I reach the stem from the vine.
My knowledge of apples and carrots tell me this is as far as I should consume.
I prop myself back on my elbows and stare up through the branches at the little scattered puzzle pieces of the sky.
I go to stretch and yawn, but I am unable to catch my breath.

I try to take a deep breath, but simply gasp.
My lips tingle and my tongue feels strange.
My heart flutters,
then stomps,
then flutters again.
My throat feels as if it has been stuffed with cotton.
I try to cry out, but only wheeze.
My lungs beg for air,
but my mouth and throat refuse to give in.
I wretch back on the ground,
grabbing my throat,
screaming internally.
They will not find my body until lunchtime.
The pain in my abdomen radiates, I'm sure I must be dying.

Guts: An Inventory of Motherhood and Abjection

Hair.
I have always had thick hair.
Long, melted chocolate layers that streamed down my back.
Duchess Raven Waves, they had called me as a child.
Duchess Raven Waves was the nemesis of Lady Lovely Locks,
the blonde-haired heroine from my favourite childhood cartoon.
Pregnancy had only enhanced its fullness and luster.
By the ninth month, I looked like Brooke Shields in the 1980's Calvin Klein ad.
Once my progeny was evicted from my womb,
my hair became weak and flat.
First, I noticed heavier clumps in my hairbrush.
Our shower drain clogged.
Our sink drain followed.
The hair fell out with ease.
The wind would blow,
and strands would fly away.
I hoped no one notices the blotches of exposed skin that now reveal the many moles I have on my head.
My mother had told me they were there,
but I had never known if it was true until now.

Breasts.
These were the breasts I had always wanted.
They came with a price.
Two days after I was once again the only living creature inhabiting my body,
my milk came in.
I looked in the mirror and saw the breasts I had dreamt of in junior high.

Large and full and firm and perky.
And sore.
So fucking sore.
With dark areolas and deep blue veins that bled out from the center.
They were hard as rocks and lumpy.
I did not recognize them as my own.
They did not look like my breasts.
They did not feel like my breasts.
They leaked constantly.
They would leak whenever I felt anything.
If I watched a sad commercial on tv,
they would leak.
If they rearranged something in the grocery store and I got slightly confused,
they would leak.
If a song came on the radio that reminded me of my childhood,
they would leak.
Anything that made me feel remotely human would cause surges of fluid to expel from my breasts and leak through my shirt.
My large, full breasts.
My beautiful nightmare.

Stomach.
I remember the flatness.
I used to be so smooth.
I looked like an after picture from a weight loss ad.
I worked so fucking hard to look that way.
I walked everywhere.
I went to yoga;
sometimes twice a day.
I ate so much cauliflower.
Now the skin falls. Sags.
It is loose around my belly button.
Pink claw marks drag down my skin.
"They're your tiger stripes!" the mommy bloggers proudly proclaim.
They're my battles scars, I say to myself.

Who owns this stomach?
It was once so flat.
Then it protruded from my body like a tumour.
Now it sags.
It sags out over the too tight line of my underwear.
It sags out over my thighs when I sit.
I do not remember having this much skin,
and yet…
there it is.

Scent.
I will never forget this smell.
My body, cut open and expelled a six-pound womb creature,
followed by blood and guts and feces.
I screamed and cried and begged for it to stop.
Then they put some stitches between my hatchet wound and my asshole and told me it was over.
They gave me some mesh underwear,
like the ones my incontinent grandmother wears.
Before I was able to think straight, they made me stand up and go to the bathroom.
One nurse handed me a squirt bottle.
You'll need to keep this. You need to fill it with warm water and squirt it on your vagina every day.
She sends me into the bathroom and closes the door.
The smell is overwhelming.
My vagina reeks of afterbirth.
This is what my insides smell like.
A week passes, but the smell does not fade.
Not even a little.
Every day I sit on the toilet and it fills with blood.
Then I squirt warm water all over my swollen vagina,
and I am physically attacked by the smell of my insides.
I wonder if this is what a ripped open dead body would smell like.
The irony is not lost on me.

**David Doesn't Live Here Anymore; or
How to Make the World's Best Banana Bread**

Hey everyone! Welcome back to *Fab Eats with Farrah*! Today, I wanted to share a timeless classic with you: Banana bread with toasted walnuts. I know, I know, you are all probably thinking "Ummm, Farrah, literally every food blogger out there has a recipe for banana bread!" And you would be correct. But this recipe is truly something special, and I wanted to share it with you! Following this recipe will you give THEEEE moistest, tenderest, most delicious banana bread you have ever tasted. I am not messing around. This truly is a guide to making the world's best banana bread.

First things first, I can't take credit for this recipe. I wish I could, but I'm an honest woman, so I have to give credit where credit is due. This recipe belonged to a woman named Odette. I say "belonged" because Odette is long dead (RIP Odette!). I didn't actually know Odette very well, but I *did* know her grandson, David, *suuuuuper* well, so I guess it's kind of thanks to him that I got my hands on this amazing recipe!

David was actually my first boyfriend, if you consider ninth grade boyfriends real (I totally do!). I guess he was sort of my first love, and he was really close with his grandmother, the late, great Odette. So, David was my first love. I wrote his name on all of my underwear in sharpie just like Kirsten Dunst did with Josh Hartnett in that movie where she kills herself because she's super sad but still looks really pretty. David would break up with me, then I would date someone else, then David would get mad, so we'd get back together, then David would get a crush on someone who looked way more like Kirsten Dunst than I did, so we'd break up again, but then that girl wouldn't like David, but another boy would like me, and David would get jealous and call me a slut, blah blah blah, you know how it goes. Junior high, am I right?

David always had a crush on a new girl. She was always blonde, and she always had bigger boobs than me. He'd decide he *loved* this new girl, so he'd break up with me, but we would stay best friends because I really, really understood him, you know? We'd talk for hours about how much he *loooooved* his new girlfriend and how perfect she was and how hot she was, and I would be really supportive because I was such a good best friend. But those girls would always break up with him and he would always come back to me. I don't think those other girls understood him like I did. David was very complex, and not like other guys our age. David read Brett Easton Ellis, and listened to a lot of classic punk rock, and thought everyone else was just too stupid and phony.

David and I dated on and off all through high school. He was literally my first everything. And I mean *everything*. Do you ever look back on your life in high school and just cringe? Like, David and I always had sex with porn on in the background, and he would always make me act out whatever Jenna Jameson was doing in whatever video he put on (Jenna was his fave). Gross, right? I feel like I've seen Jenna Jameson naked more times than I've seen myself naked lol. *Sigh* the things we do for love! David could be such a weirdo, but he could also be really sweet. He would make me mix CDs all the time. They were mostly really crude songs by like Nine Inch Nails and the Bloodhound Gang, but it was still sweet. David just had this really dark sense of humour.

At the end of senior year, David and I were in one of our "off" phases, which meant we were still having sex, but he was allowed to try and fuck other people, but I wasn't. I think we've all been there lol. Anyway, I ended up getting pregnant, and OF COURSE David said it wasn't his because everyone knew I was a huge slut (he could be so dramatic sometimes). Once he got over calling me a whore, he was like "Ok, cool, well if you're pregnant then you need to get an abortion." So, of course, I did. David borrowed Odette's car (RIP Odette!) and took me to get one but didn't even wait for me to finish! I had to legit get a cab home from my own senior year abortion! And then David wouldn't even go to prom with me! Don't even get me started on that one!

After that, David went off to a college in Halifax and I stayed in town. A girlfriend of mine went to the same college as David and told me that his name had been written on several "shit lists" in various women's bathroom stalls in several college bars. If you don't know what a shit list is, it's kind of this thing women do to keep each other safe. You write a shit list on the wall in the girl's bathroom and other women can add names to it. David was probably added because he is dramatic as HELL and that mood is 100% worth avoiding. Anyway, once David moved away, I never really heard from him again. I'd send him the occasional e-mail to check in, but I assume he probably stopped using his old e-mail and just stuck with his new college e-mail. Whatever, it was fine. I moved on. Years passed, I got into blogging and vlogging, and David, as far as I could tell, never jumped on board with the whole social media thing.

So anyway, a couple of years back I had heard through the grapevine that David's sweet grandmother Odette had died and left him her house (he was always so spoiled!), so he had come back to St. John's for a few months to fix it up so he could sell it.

I literally had zero interest in attempting to see David while he was back in town. Don't get me wrong, I looked fantastic. I was 25 and THRIVING. I did NOT peak in high school, you know what I'm saying? Anyway, as luck would have it, I actually ran into David at a bar one night. We chatted for a bit, and he invited me over for dinner. David had lost his youthful luster (and a weird amount of hair for only 25), but I still accepted the invitation. He still had a soft spot in my heart, and I guess I was interested in seeing what he had done with Odette's place.

I hadn't been in David's grandmother's house in maybe a decade. All of her things were tossed into boxes haphazardly and without any care. Aside from a few old scenic paintings and her collection of dog statues, Odette's entire life had been thoughtlessly tossed into boxes. I didn't know David's grandmother well, but I always remembered how into dogs she was. She had these super heavy dog statues lining her fireplace. They were about 2 feet tall and 20 pounds each. They were scary lifelike.

She had a German Sheppard, a Cocker Spaniel, a Beagle, a dog I wasn't all that familiar with, one of those Lassie dogs, and a Golden Retriever. When I walked in, they all stared up at me with their glazed over, black eyes, which really gave me the creeps.

Dinner was tragic. David ordered a lousy pizza with green pepper on it (I hate green pepper and have been vocal about this my entire life) and bought some disgusting cheap red wine. I sat, picking the peppers off a greasy slice of pizza, and David snickered, and asked if I had always been so picky.

"I dated you for four years," I said, "so I guess not."

The thing about green peppers is that even if you take them off something, you can still taste that they've been there. The bad taste doesn't go away.

David had clearly had a few drinks before I arrived, and almost immediately began regaling me with stories about his college experience. All the big tits and fake blonds and "real sluts, you remember the kind?" I guess I did remember the kind.

Had he always talked about women like this?

He had, hadn't he?

As I sipped my awful glass of wine, David began to steer the conversation towards our time together in high school. I wish I could say he was subtle with his innuendos, but I don't know that "subtle" was in David's vocabulary. Yes, I remembered him fucking me while pressing my face into a pillow and staring at a video of Chasey Lain getting fucked in the ass. Yes, I remember the time he "accidentally" came in my eye. Everyone at school knew about that one by Monday morning. How could I forget?

I remembered everything, except why I had any sort of soft spot for David.

As he went on and on about our wild times together, David leaned over and began to rub my knee. I sipped my wine. Then he traveled from my knee to my thigh. I pushed his hand down, but he pushed it right back. "You look so great, Farrah," he said, "You really do. I really didn't think I'd be attracted to you when I came home, but you look really hot."

Do other men actually talk like that? Is that what they think constitutes as a compliment? Seriously, I would love to know.

I laughed. I didn't know what else to do. For as long as I could remember, David lived on a pedestal in my head. He was my first everything. And now here he was, and it was like I was seeing him for the first time.

David leaned in and kissed my neck. I froze. An unfamiliar sensation went through my body, but it was kind of like right before I got my first pap smear. His hand reached up and began to grope my right breast. The breast he had once told me was too small, but I could probably get my tits done someday. I pushed his hand away. "Come on, Farrah," he laughed, putting his hand back. "No, David," I said sternly, pushing him away. I had never said "no" to David before, and prior to that moment, I could never imagine myself saying it, either.

David was visibly drunk and definitely shocked, because it was like he didn't hear me at all. He tried to pin me against the chair and bit down on my neck, so I lifted my left knee up and pushed him off. He fell back and I stood up and adjusted my dress. "Fuck off, David," I grumbled, rolling my eyes. I began to turn away when David pushed me down from behind. My face slammed into Odette's beige shag carpet, which smelled like dried cat piss. I could feel David pin his body weight on top of me, and without hesitation he began to pull up the bottom of my dress. Even though I had never been in a situation like that before, the whole thing felt weirdly familiar. My body didn't even try to fight him off. It was like the whole thing seemed…normal. But I wasn't 17 anymore. And I guess I knew this wasn't normal.

I looked to my side and saw those creepy fucking dogs staring back at me. With a force I didn't know I had in me, I pulled all my weight to the right and David fell off me. Quickly, I grabbed the first dog I could get my hands on: the Golden Retriever. Before I could even think, I swung it at David's head.

I broke my leg once at camp when I was 12. I was running down the wharf to jump in the lake and slipped and fell onto one of the beams holding the damn thing up, then tumbled into the water in an awkward position. I heard the bone in my leg crack. It was disgusting. But you know what's even more disgusting? Hearing a skull crack open.

David's head swerved and fell onto his grandmother's ugly, baby shit green couch. He made a weird gurgling noise, and, at first, I was scared to look. But, after a minute, I womaned up and turned around. There he was: my first love, brains bashed in by his grandmother's Golden Retriever statue. Skull and brain fragments strewn across her blood-soaked couch. I sat and watched for a bit. I thought about calling 911, but I guess I just didn't. After 5 minutes—which felt like an eternity—David was dead. That was it. He was just gone.

I wasn't really sure what to do, so I got some garbage bags from the kitchen. First, I wrapped one around his head to deal with all the brain and blood ooze. Then I wrapped up the rest of his body. I remembered that Odette had one of those old, shitty, unfinished basements that still had a dirt floor, and—lucky for me—the old bag never got that finished. I dug in the basement until 4 in the morning, then I dragged David and the couch cushions in and covered up the hole. I put on an old pair of cleaning gloves and brought down old boxes of Odette's things and some dry wall that had been torn down for renovations. I tossed it all over the basement floor to make it look like David had just been throwing garbage down there. Honestly, it was pretty crafty if I do say so myself.

By the time I cleaned myself up I realized it was almost noon. I got all my shit together and decided to take the Golden Retriever statue for good measure. While I was getting my car keys off the kitchen counter, I noticed an old notebook with "recipes" written across the front, and for some reason I decided to take that, too.

I opened the front door to leave, and there she was: a girl who looked barely legal. A girl who probably wasn't legal. She had blonde hair and a push up bra and overlined lips. She was exactly the kind of girl David liked. She was a sexy child.

"Oh," she said, surprised to see me. "Is David here?" she asked.

"No," I responded, smiling. "David doesn't live here anymore."

After she left, I walked out and closed the door behind me, blood-stained Golden Retriever in hand.

Anyway, I got home and looked through the recipe book, which I guess had belonged to David's grandmother for a long time. She had recorded all of her favourite recipes. That's where I found this banana bread recipe, and let me tell you, it is to DIE for.

Oh my gosh, that pun wasn't even intended.

**My Heart is as Deep as the Ocean
and My Sorrows Have Filled it with Tears.**

I didn't want anyone to read my poems,
because poems were such a juvenile, feminine thing to do.
Every teenage girl had a book of poems.
Sonnets about 13-year-old boys named Brandon,
and Haikus about getting our first period.
Rhythmically lining out our fears,
hopes,
and desires,
alongside our favourite Spice Girls' lyrics.
Young girls are always so dramatic!
Our parents and teachers would always say.
Girls are too emotional. They take everything so seriously.
The boys in our class would groan, rolling their eyes,
as if the public mockery of the blood on our white jeans had not been
worthy of tears.
For what do we allow girls their tears?
Perhaps when our tongues swell and pus with infection from a lifetime
of biting them.
Then our hyperbolic feminine nature will not be so juvenile.
Maybe some day we won't build up dams,
because, like beavers, we strive to keep things contained.
Then I will write of my tears,
and I will not be ashamed that I have written them into existence.
I will not think it silly to rhyme *cry* and *dry*,
or *try* and *die*.
I will not think only sad and ugly girls complain in stanzas.
I will not use the word "complain"
to describe another woman's pain.
I will allow the weight of my heart to be immeasurable,

and I will fill it with all of the tears and storms and bitten tongues that have filled me for so long.
When it breaks, my tears will flow out,
and I will patch it back together with band-aids
featuring pictures of Disney princesses.
Snow White will hold together the left and right atrium,
while Ariel re-attaches my pulmonary vein.
I will fill each room with my voice,
my dramatics,
my reactions.
I will read my poems in coffee shops and on street corners.
I will tattoo my words on my body,
down my back,
so to see me nude is to see me naked.
I will love bigger than a blue whale.
And when people say I'm being hyperbolic
I will say it is a shame they are not in love with anyone.
I will be juvenile and feminine and theatrical.
I will paint my nails the brightest pink,
and tell people there is something so important about the colour a woman chooses to paints her nails.

The Vicious Kind

Our neighbourhood was quiet and dreamy.
The sun shone every day,
and, somehow, there was always the right number of clouds in the sky.
Each house was uniquely different,
yet perfectly the same.
The grass was immaculately manicured,
and an appropriate amount of wind could often be found blowing
through the elm trees that lined every lawn.
My sister and I would watch *Sleeping Beauty* on lazy Sunday mornings,
eating cereal in our nightdresses in front of the television,
moving only when father told us to go put more clothes on because his
friends were coming over.
We'd retreat from the house to avoid the men,
and settle on the concreate porch to cover our toenails in sparkling pink,
and shimmering turquoise.
The older boys whose voices had begun to deepen would whistle at us
as they walked by,
laughing their own private jokes to one another.
My stomach would grow tight from my awareness of my body,
and its ability to be gazed upon.

I had just turned twelve.
My sister was ten.
The boy next door would pull her long blonde braids,
and shoot spitballs at her from behind our joint fence.
He just likes you,
our mother would say,
as she watched the attack while hanging wet clothes on the line.
When the smallest hint of breasts appeared on my chest
my mother bought me a training bra.

It was uncomfortably tight on my shoulders,
but mother said I was too old and not wearing one would be indecent.
My sister and I would giggle at the kitchen table, making faces at one another.
She would chew up a glob of potato and open her mouth to show me.
My father would look to my mother with disgust,
and mother would promptly tell us that our behaviour wasn't ladylike.
Is anything a girl does ladylike?

The same older boy who had whistled
snapped my ill-fitting bra strap while I checked the mail.
I ran home and screamed into my pillow,
burying the constrictive scoundrel deep in my laundry basket.
The next day, while lying in the grass of my backyard,
watching the sun splinter through the trees,
my nemesis and his friends returned.
While his underlings held me down,
their zit-faced leader stole my sneakers and ran,
flinging them over our neighbour's fence.
The sneakers were a pointless gesture.
He hadn't really stolen them from me,
he'd just moved them.
The restraint, however, had been another thing.
That night I heard my parents having a heated discussion about my behaviour.
She brings this on herself,
my father had said.
Well, I told her she needs to be wearing a bra now,
my mother argued, as if she was also on trial for my crime of existence.

My sister had gone ahead of me to the small park on our suburban street.
When I arrived,
she was crying
as the boys taunted her
dangling her beloved stuffed rabbit above her tiny blonde head.

Give it back,
I demanded as they laughed.
Give it back!
I roared,
as my small fist crashed into his nose.
He dropped the rabbit,
and we took advantage of the shock to flee to the confines of our home.
His blood was smeared across my knuckles.
I locked myself in the bathroom,
and licked myself clean.

The next day,
I saw it.
While riding my bike on the trail behind our house.
Spray painted on the cement.
Paint being more permanent and official than chalk.
Lilith Martin is a slut!
with my home phone number underneath.
I was under attack,
and yet,
my parents were mad at me for those obscene and anonymous phone calls
that plagued dinner that night.
Are you trying to get yourself a reputation?
She must be doing something for someone to write something like that!
I'm not doing anything,
I argue to no one.
My sister takes my hand underneath the table.
The sound of my parents fades away,
and I think of the taste of copper on my tongue.

I let a few days pass,
waiting for the other boys to grow bored of their late-night calls.
They were in high school,
it didn't take long for them to find a new insidious hobby.
Timing was everything.

My sister and I would sit in our living room window,
or graze on our front lawn.
He had to be alone.
I knew what he wanted,
and I knew if I could catch him alone,
and offer myself up,
he'd take it.
On a bright Tuesday morning,
we spotted him.
All alone,
heading onto the trail across the street.
I followed him from a distance at first,
my wrists crossed behind my back.
After a few minutes
I decided to get closer.
I needed him to notice me.
He stopped.
Turned.
What do you want?
I want what you want.
I approach slowly,
and he says nothing.
I get close enough so he can smell my mother's perfume,
and my strawberry lip balm.
I smile,
and lightly giggle as my stomach rumbles.
When my lips touch his he doesn't move,
not at first.
After what could have been an eternity,
he slips a hand around my waist and begins to kiss me back.
The moment is meaningless.
My heart only begins to truly race when I clench my teeth onto his bottom lip.
His blood fills both our mouths;
he begins to scream.
He starts to call me a crazy bitch,

but I draw the rock from behind my back before he can finish.
Blood streams down his temple,
and suddenly I'm on him.
Ravenous.
This is what you wanted,
I whisper,
before devouring his lips and the tip of his tongue.
I return home,
content.
His blood drying to my mouth and chin,
trailing down my tank top,
staining the little blue flowers.
What the hell is wrong with you?!
What have you done?!
Mother and Father shout.
I see my sister in the corner and smile at her,
unashamed,
unafraid.
Let them yell and scream and blame,
as we feast on their hearts in front of the fireplace.

The Afterparty

What do you call the gathering after a funeral?
I asked my mother.
It isn't a wake.
And I've never heard it called a gathering.
Usually, it's at a family members house,
whoever owns the biggest home.
Even if they don't want to host,
their domestic space proves to be a necessity in the aftermath of grief.
A few times I've attended these gatherings at halls.
The same places we hold bridal and baby showers.
Places usually reserved for the celebration of beginnings.
My mother says this gathering is called a reception,
because the family gathers to receive sympathy.
But that's so odd.
Every funeral reception I have attended had food and conversation and various types of alcohol.
Aunts running around laying out trays of snowballs and egg salad sandwiches,
which I assume you have to be over fifty to enjoy.
At my grandmother's funeral,
I posed for several pictures with my younger brother.
Those were the nicest pictures we had ever taken together,
and one of them is framed and sits on my bookshelf.
Our smiles are authentic,
and our skin is tanned.
It was a beautiful,
sunny Friday afternoon,
and my brother is holding a beer.
How odd it is to say,
Oh, that picture was taken at our grandmother's funeral reception.

Reception feels like the wrong word.
The family truly receives sympathy and condolences during the wake.
The "sorrys" always run out by the time the funeral is over.
Once the body is in the ground,
people are tired.
They want to be fed food from toothpicks,
and offered wine from a box.
They want to talk about local events,
their current ailments,
and accidental family gossip.
They want to drink beer from coolers on the deck,
and discuss recent hockey trades.
As if those they mourn were just in the next room.
Or had never existed at all.
What do you call a gathering where you go to forget?
To talk about anything else.
To eat and drink,
then go home and think,
That's the end of that, then.
As if an entire life can be tied up and finished over rum and coke.
As if grief is completed once the last meatball has been consumed.
As if one afterparty can conclude a life.

White Curtains

I've been dreaming a lot about when I was a child. Maybe eight or nine-years-old. We lived at 8 Berry Street, and an older woman named Shirley lived next door in number 10. She was a widower who had become close with my grandmother. In the dream, I go knock on Shirley's door, but she doesn't answer. I hear children playing in the backyard, just like I remember from when I was a kid.

Shirley had three grandchildren who would stay with her for two weeks in the summer. The boy's name was Chris; he was a year younger than me, and we used to play together. I go around to the back of the house and Shirley is on the veranda, looking down at several little girls running and laughing in the yard. I can't make out their faces. I call out to Shirley, expecting her to remember me.

She looks down towards me and gives me the oddest look. She looks up towards my house, and I follow her gaze. I see the window in the back: my grandmother's room. The window is open and her white lace curtains are blowing out. I see someone in the window, but before I can tell who it is, I always wake up.

I've been having strange dreams about white lace curtains since I was about six. When I was five and my brother, Robbie, was nine we had a babysitter, Issie Andrews, who was fourteen. Robbie thought he was too old to have a babysitter, but he didn't mind Issie because she was kind of like this cool, older kid. She cut her hair short, she played street hockey, and could kick his ass in video games. Robbie loved her and so did I.

She would read me *Nancy Drew* books and even let me watch *Unsolved Mysteries* sometimes even though mom and dad typically didn't allow it. My mother said Issie was a late-bloomer, but at five I had no idea what that meant.

About six months after Issie started babysitting us, something changed. She let her hair grow down to her shoulders and would occasionally wear make-up. I stopped seeing her playing street hockey with the guys out on Noad Place, her cul-de-sac which was right by my street.

One day I overheard Robbie telling Mikey Price that our babysitter was hot now that she had boobs and brushed her hair. It wasn't long after that that Issie stopped babysitting us and I stopped seeing her around the neighbourhood. I remember asking my dad what happened to Issie, to which he nonchalantly replied: "I'm sure she's around." It was never really brought up again.

One day, I rode my bike past Issie's house and noticed that the curtains in her bedroom window had been replaced. Where there had once been deep purple curtains with large gold stars, there now hung old-fashioned white lace curtains just like my grandmother had in her room.
I never saw Issie again.

True Newfoundlander

I have never gutted a fish.
For that matter, I've never even been fishing.
Yet the smell of cod clings to my identity,
a stench I've neither earned nor deserve.
My grandfather didn't fish or farm.
He worked at the Coke bottle factory
over on Kenmount Road.
It might not have been Kenmount Road, though.
The factory shut down before my time.

My grandmother never knit square wash cloths for her neighbours,
or made pea soup with hearty chunks of salt beef.
Instead, she washed the bedding of those who came from away
and stayed the night at the old Newfoundland Hotel.
From the hotel windows she would look out
at a downtown that reflected back a street of bars
and rows of boats.

It wasn't until after my grandmother died that I learned she'd written
poetry in her youth,
or that she used to love drawing horses.
I can't picture her girlhood in rural Newfoundland.
How could I,
when I've never been further than Northern Bay Sands?
I know little of confederation,
and whose side my family was on.
Did we cheer for Joey Smallwood?
Or call him a villain?
My grandmother had still been around the bay when he won,
she'd been fourteen.

Had she cared at all?
Had she been passionate about politics?

At sixteen she would run into a burning house to save her infant niece.
She got out with a mason jar of her sister's family savings.
My grandmother didn't own any shoes,
but at eighteen, she got her first moose.
Am I less of a Newfoundlander than my grandmother because I've never seen a moose?
I've tasted it, but only at a fine dining restaurant downtown.
It cost me $68 and was drizzled in a sauce I cannot pronounce.
Would Nan have laughed at this?

I found out about my grandmother's attempt to save her niece during the eulogy at her funeral.
The young live on the backs of tragedies they never felt.
Grandmothers and granddaughters,
But grandfathers and grandsons as well.
We feel the weight of the Newfoundland we never knew.
When the fishery was open, before the coal mines shut down.
Before the oxycodone came in to soothe our worn bodies,
mangled from cold early mornings deep in the earth or out at sea.

"You don't sound like a Newfoundlander,"
is the most frequent compliment I receive when I am away from home.
"What does a Newfoundlander sound like?"
I ask,
knowing it's a question I myself cannot answer.

Male Gaze

The first summer I lived on Victoria Street,
I'd go to The Ship every night hoping I'd see you.
In the evenings,
when I'd get ready to go out
I'd leave my curtains wide open
because I thought the boy who lived across the street might be attractive.
I wasn't sure if he was,
but there's always a chance.
A chance to be seen through the crowd at The Ship,
or noticed across the way,
standing in a lilac bra in a bedroom window.
For who am I in this town if I'm not seen by you?
Or any man, for that matter.
When I imagine my life in my head,
I can skateboard,
and play bass guitar.
I play my own shows at The Ship
and you all come to see me sing the most beautiful words you've ever heard.
I'm a female Bob Dylan
with a face that doesn't belong in such a small city.
In my imagination,
every boy I've ever known goes to the theatre to watch this documentary about me.
Because that's all a mind is,
a documentary we make about ourselves.
And they're all in awe of me.
They adore me.
I'm everyone's "one that got away."
I'm the dream girl across the bar.

I'm the mystery woman in the window on Victoria Street.
A St. John's icon of beauty and grace.
I wonder, from my window,
and from that seat at The Ship,
if every girl craves that gaze
and dreams about that admiration.
I look for other girls
in other downtown windows,
changing with the curtains open.
And hope I'm not alone.

The Author

Krysta Fitzpatrick is an educator and writer from St. John's, Newfoundland. She is currently teaching in both the English and Gender Studies Departments of Memorial University.

She resides in Mount Pearl with her husband, two sons, mother, and beloved dog Dipper.

Manufactured by Amazon.ca
Bolton, ON